HOW I
BECAME
POOR

HOW UNFASHIONABLE IT IS BEING POOR
IN THE
TWENTY FIRST CENTURY

HOW I BECAME POOR

PHARAOH XAVIER

HOW I BECAME POOR
HOW UNFASHIONABLE IT IS BEING POOR

iUniverse books may be ordered through booksellers or by contacting:

iUniverse
1663 Liberty Drive
Bloomington, IN 47403
www.iuniverse.com
1-800-Authors (1-800-288-4677)

Because of the dynamic nature of the Internet, any web addresses or links contained in this book may have changed since publication and may no longer be valid. The views expressed in this work are solely those of the author and do not necessarily reflect the views of the publisher, and the publisher hereby disclaims any responsibility for them.

Any people depicted in stock imagery provided by Getty Images are models, and such images are being used for illustrative purposes only.
Certain stock imagery © Getty Images.

ISBN: 978-1-5320-7469-1 (sc)
ISBN: 978-1-5320-7470-7 (e)

Print information available on the last page.

iUniverse rev. date: 09/11/2019

There was at one time that poor people with real life issues were fodder for talk shows and subject matter for print. Now that the upper middle class has expanded with there ability to purchase home, cars, pools, kids, HDTV 30 and up inch big screen TVs. These are now the new generation of problematic poor people, the over extenders, lets call them. People living over their limits causing them to fall into debt which will bring on a whole slew of old, new issues that civilized people in the twenty first century finds palatable especially for talk shows.

Middle class peoples get bumped up and poor people get bumped down or bumped off completely. Why

would the nation want to be reminded that there is an underclass that exist and needs help. People have this idea that all poor people like being poor and living off the system. That may be true for a very, very small portion of us, but generally that's not the case.

Take me for example; some people are born with a silver spoon in their mouth while other is born with a rusted shovel in hand. I'm one of those people.

Though I'm unable to work full or part time work, it didn't start out that way. Being poor like this has limited me to doors given to those more privileged. Now I write, hoping that at least my life story will mean something to someone, someday. Maybe prevent somebody from making those wrong choices I've made that's lead me to this point in my life.

When I was a younger, healthier man, I started working at the age of 15 in a butcher's shop. Held a job up until the age of 40, I'm now 41. Everything I've ever had I struggled to obtain, so believe my when I say that I took nothing for granted. I worked jobs that were back breaking and environmentally cruel.

Like working the lanes for New Jersey's state car inspection station. Imagine working in ninety degree

heat in the summer and thirty and below degrees in the winter. Winter's snow, slush and cold, angry customers having their inspection date during the worst months and forced to bring their cars in to get inspected. As bad as it was for them think what we on the lanes had to endure while all the time smiling and being pleasant while freezing our asses off or frying during summer. Never the less the job got done, with blistering winds barreling through the inside lane or just plain outdoor exposure with no real shelter except for metal booths, try sticking your tongue on metal in dead winter, now try staying warm in a box made out of one. Yea, you got it; nothing you put on kept you warm. Two thermal under wears, three pairs of socks, sweatpants, thick uniform shirt, sweater, jacket, scarf, winter uniform coat, skully, uniform hat with flaps, two to three pairs of gloves, uniform boots and a extra scarf to wrap around over your nose. All this and a little metal booth with a dysfunctional space heater. I worked the lanes for five years until I fell upon hard times.

I had lost everything to drugs, so I went and joined the army, at least I tried, came to find out I was HIV positive. They said no and I was faced with telling my mom and siblings about my findings. At first I was

relieved because this meant I had to be careful now when having sex, but now to tell moms the good news. Told mom not long after I found out myself, she took it much as I expected.

I had to make sure I washed every plate, cup and utensil with bleach water, but that grew into the idea of me buying my own dish ware. Aaaah yes, I saw were this was heading to, dealing with the fear fueled by news reports and misinformation, I didn't hold it over my moms head, but what do I do now? Here I am 29 jobless and infected with the HIV virus? Not finding work in a small town of Plainfield wasn't setting well with dear mom, especially when she wanted her rent money. No one lived for free in moms home except for young children, but not if you're her daughter with kids, you had to pay for them as well.

For me a single person living with just mom meant get a job fast. I tried to find a job that could support myself and get mom her rent. So I looked towards New York City if you can, you know the rest. Well, with her permission to use her car I drove to Newark New Jersey and found I couldn't afford to park it in a lot so I parked it in a McDonald's parking lot, just for the day, but when I got back, guess what? They were towing my mom's car

away! I freaked, panic was in the air, I begged, pleaded, but they couldn't care less, heartless parasites. Oh man, I'm fucked, I couldn't go back home with out her car, she'll rip out my heart and sell it to get the money, at least that's what I believed.

There I stood no home and no money. I think in all the haze of fear I called my brother Steven to come and get me. He talked it out with mom for me I think, by telling her there's a job at Newark Airport. It was security watch at the gate for delivery trucks DHL I think. I got the job, my brother would pick me up, oh, and did I mention that it was a night job during the winter!

Sitting in a hallowed out school bus position at the gate, with no heater. I knew I had to take it to make enough money to get moms car out of the pound lot. Fortunately a security position opened up at Tri Ways security office further in Newark Airport which I eventually got. It was detaining illegal immigrant sneaking in on flights into the U.S.

Mom eventually got her car back and I had a job making great money. Unfortunately the job counted on illegal getting caught and detained. This meant no work if none were caught, but when there was work we worked 24 hour shifts. When work slowed to a halt, mom got

edgy about her rent. I told her it's worth me sticking it out, but all she wanted was her rent. Arguments grew worst and finally came to a head. She felt I didn't understand to her needs and I felt she was bullying me into a choice to make. She took back her extra set of car keys and I stuck to my guns and stood firm. Either find a local job or get out! Well, I in good conscience left to my convictions so after the blow out of all blow outs I packed a duffle bag and tied my uniform coat to it and walked the dead man walking march to the front door. Stopping at the living room entrance there she sat not moving an inch frozen in time. Fear over took me, I didn't know what her next move or thought would be to respond to me choice to leave her alone in that big house. I had made up my mind to leave no matter what she said. I took two steps towards the front door, she spoke startling me, here, she spoke, and "all I have is five dollars." I took it and thanked her. I headed for the door all the while her eyes stayed on me watching me leave. I knew I wasn't safe until I reached the street. I saw the front gate leading to the street and once beyond the gates I knew there was no going back.

I laid all my trust in God that he would guide me and watch over me in my attempt to become a man and

own up to my own responsibilities. I headed toward the highway on route 22 walking all the way. I approach a train trestle and noticed some kids out the corner of my eye. As I continued walking, I heard clicking noises behind me, I turned around and caught the two boys and a girl pitching stones at me; I yelled at them and they took off running. I almost started to cry thinking could this be an omen to what awaits? For a second I thought to turn around to a sure thing but I had developed a strong faith in God and decided to trust in him.

I was determined to make it to that job 30-40 miles away. I said to myself I would prove your faith no matter what. So reaching the highway I walked while cars whisked by me, afraid, one might take me out. After a while I started to not care as the light faded and darkness took over. By the time I reached a White Castle it was pitch black out lit only by the stores along the highway. I was tired and hungry and debated whether to spend the five and eat or hitch a ride and eat later once I reach my job. This meant going hungry for that night. Instead a thought entered my head making me aware that I made it to Union where my brother Steve lived. I got food and change and called him from a pay phone, told him what occurred and what choice I made. He came and

found me at the burger place and road me the rest of the way there. He didn't have any money on hand but I was more than grateful for the lift. I walked into the building which Tri Ways shared with an airport taxi service. As Steven drove off I knew this was it, a true test of faith. I walked in and walked to the conference room used my duffle bag as a pillow and my coat as cover and slept there that night.

Being that I had airport clearance again a thought came into my head, go hang out in the airport. So I went to the bathroom washed up in the sink and caught the tram to one of the terminals. I walked around that terminal wondering what to do. I began praying to myself almost to the point of tears, but I had to believe that my God would take care of me. I had no money to by food or anything to drink but water. So I wondered around until I heard a voice calling me, I thought who's calling me here? I'm looking around trying to see who's calling me. At first I thought it was my imagination, but the voice directed me to look where it was coming from and like an angel sent from God, there before my eyes was my closet friend from high school Cheryl Williams, I think that's her last name. Anyway, forgive me Cheryl, when I saw her I almost busted out

in tears. She was working at the airport too driving the electric car picking up folks and taking them to their destination. She had no one at that moment and told me to hop on, we recanted our high school days to the present and I told her my situation. Thinking she'd lend my some money to eat instead directed me to earn my own cash doing wheel chair pick ups.

At that moment an intercom call for six wheel chair sky caps pick up at a flight something, something so Cheryl said hang on. We sped over to the flight, she yell grab a wheel chair and since I had security clearance I was able to pick up a passenger and take them to where their vehicle was parked. I smiled at Cheryl and she smiled back. Mind you helping people from or to their destinations doesn't guarantee a financial gratitude for your service so all I could do was hope for the best. He was a frail old man who spoke about his flight; we talked all the way to the underground parking area to the park vehicles in the outside parking lot. Once we got to their vehicle, oh I forgot he was accompanied by a nurse I think, anyway I offered to help with getting him in the vehicle and pack their bags in the trunk but the old man was adamant about not helping. So he shook my hand and thanked me for the service and talks and said not to

worry and I took the wheel chair back to the terminal. I noticed a folded bill in my hand left by the kind old man. It was folded tight so I couldn't tell how much it was. Once in the terminal I unfolded it and to my surprise it was a twenty dollar bill. I almost screamed I was so happy. I found Cheryl and told her what happened she told me about an employee lunchroom down stairs where the meals were huge and cheap and yes I ate like a king that night. After that day I stayed at the airport and God supplied the jobs I needed to sustain me there until worked at the security office picked up.

I could continue on that part of my life and how it turned out but I need to stay on track about the reason for this letter. I made some bad choice during those times which lead me to moving to New York the Bronx. Even with the HIV growing inside me I kept working until I began to tire easily. A friend helped me seek medical attention and I felled onto being considered disable by the medical doctors. I ended up in the system and there I've been since.

But my spirit never left me to feel helpless so instead of working a job, my friend and I did odd and end work as well as volunteering for GMHC. Years would pass and

our friendship would turn volatile and I was left to find my way around on my own in the Bronx.

I got housing and furniture and a stable environment and searched for possible income not affecting my health. But over the years I found myself ending up in the hospital sick with fever, the doctors at Montifiore hospital ran every test possible on me. Spinal Taps, antibiotics 24 hour care to determined the cause, but came up unknown. I would recover eventually and was let go, but ended up back in due to stress triggers. This didn't stop me from finding ways to help others with hiv/aids or educating my communities of color.

I started with my housing agency V.O.A helping my case manager Mickey, who was the best case manager I ever had with field trip and outings which lead to working For The Bronx hiv/aids care network which lead to GMAD and the advocacy group state wide and ended up finally at Harlem United. I was told they had a part position in a gay men outreach program called Hitting It Safer. Getting the position I excelled at my task, by now there were better meds to deal with the virus that made me feel strong enough to try and endure working a real job. I worked out on the streets with my Coe-worker, name omitted, walking the streets

educating and handing out condom packs to help stem the tied of spreading the virus.

Four months into the job I got paid the normal part time pay but one day I got called into conference and was told I was being overly paid. That I was actually supposed to be paid stipend payment, which meant my pay was reduce from two hundred and forty nine dollars every two weeks to a hundred and twenty nine dollars every two weeks. This puzzled me to no end, I couldn't figure out how they could do this legally, but to keep the position I had to sign a letter stating I would not pursue any charges and the repayment would be expelled. So now I was working the same work and hours for no money. I decided to hang in there since I grew to love the job and all of the workers and clients. So work harder, get paid less, a great way to get cheap labor legally. The following year our supervisor burned out from stress left and I got the pleasure filling in his position; mind you I was doing his job and my job now.

I accepted the task and excelled at it, but didn't receive any more pay unless I put in more hours. So I'd end up working on clients files and creating charts for those files and leaving work around nine o'clock at night, four hour later after closing. That came to a stop

once the CDC and the state department discovered the extra amount of pay and forced agencies to stop letting stipend works earn extra money. So all stipend workers were reduced down to earning exactly one hundred and twenty nine dollars every two weeks, but my work didn't get any less, in fact it increased.

I was running and working for four programs, filing, charting running men groups, performing in the agency's events, organization for the Aids Walk - a - thon, Gay Pride Parade and more to count. I Found time though for friends and family plus two cats, Ramseses and Pharaoh, and eventually a new relationship, but I'm getting a head of myself.

August of 2003 I remember feeling tired and achy. After doing the summer outreach at every even imaginable, beach events, as many pride events and parades, conferences and so much more to name just believe me there was a lot that summer; but in August I felt weak and tired, I just thought it was fatigue. It turned out to being over stressed which for the first time in a while I developed a raging fever and end up back at wonderful Montifiore and their amazing doctors.

With my records on hand they ran every test, but again wasn't able to find the cause. They however were

able to bring down the fever doing 24 hours care and my stay in the hospital was short. This meant getting back to work the next day or lose my job. I threw myself back into my job not really allowing myself to get rested, I couldn't afford to I was stipend worker. That meant being expendable at the whims of the employer hand.

I would after work at time go out to an eatery with a Coe - worker lets call pony, long story. At this eater I would fall in love with a marvelous man. We were just dating at first when we met but turned into the real thing after telling him my status and he so wonderfully couldn't care less. I knew he was the one, but the fairy tale romance would have a major upset. I worked hard mind you coming right out of the hospital, when in January of 2004 the fever hit again, but I didn't go to my favorite hospital as usual instead I directed my newly made boy friend to my new doctor's affiliated hospital St. Lukes Roosevelt in Manhattan.

I'll spare you every detail, but let's say one nights stay ended me up burnt from head to toes. The doctors blamed me and I blamed the hospital for locking me in a special unit with an abusive, uncaring, using the term

loosely nurse. This nurse whose ethnic back ground shall remain nameless left me lying in a hospital bed burning up with a hundred and two point four degree fever after using the call button to have her check on me cause I was shivering with cold and couldn't stop.

She finally came to my room with a really bad attitude and growled what you want. I'm shaking uncontrollably asked her to check my temperature, she did and after turned and started out my room I called to her asking what was it, she said 102.4 and turned and walked out. Thinking she would come back with either a doctor or at least something to bring down the fever and reduce the pain, all I remember passing out and waking up sometime later. All I'll say is I was unrecognizable the next day. I end up at the Cornell Burn Unit in Manhattan wrapped up like a mummy hooked up to life supporting machines with feeding tubes inserted in through my nose, I got pictures.

My new boyfriend stayed with me through it all as well as my best friends at the time and family, but mostly my friends and boy friend. They and God got me through the whole ordeal. Unfortunately nothing last forever, in short, after the staph infection and the scaring it caused the neuropathy I developed and the

depression I eventually lost all, my cheap labor hiring job, my lover, family, friends and a couple of questionable doctors.

Through all of that and so much more I felt that God might have abandoned me and life wasn't worth living, so why God I asked, why not let me die when I got burned and was told most never recover, but I did. Why did I have to go through a life of hell, from being sexually abused starting at age 6 to 18 and so much more that you would have done what I tried to last year, too? Yes, suicide, but that's another story altogether.

This is to let you know that not all poor people are degenerates, drug using crack heads, baby making machines, but some people who struggled all there life just never caught a real break. It's getting harder to keep up a positive out look when no one fucking cares. I mean really, no one cares. Since I lack the platinum colored skin to enter into the doors given to those more fortunate or been looked upon by any body outside of my friend Cheryl, and believed enough in me to take a chance in my dreams, just one chance is all I ask.

Without saying I've contacted every talk show from,

Dr. Phil, Oprah, Tyra, Montell, Maury, Rosie O'Donell blog, Judge Hatchett, The View and so on and so on. Not one called me or emailed me for show appearance, or just to find out by a simple phone call. Nope, I don't fit the criteria for day time talk shows. I, like others help kept this country running doing most of the grunt work while the rich, famous and the now upper middle class, all prospered.

So now my body isn't holding up as well, but I still feel I can contribute to society, through my words and by life's experiences, but I have no one to help me get there. The Upper and middle class has bumped the poor and working class out of the lime light, soon only the rich and famous shall rule the airwaves and all shall be considered poor, and what happens to the truly poor; I'd really hate to find out.

Recently I got mad at God cause I asked him just to speak to me and explain why is he's letting those who served mankind and him no matter what they've gone through in life to suffer? After a month of tears, heart ache, questioning God and who he is, I got no where. Not hearing from God left me dead inside wanting only to die. Hoping my essence just disperse into the cosmos and never having to live in this greed swilling, death

laden, earth killing world, but neither death nor a voice from God came.

Up until yesterday I've but gave up on God, He spoke to those in the bible, He speaks to televangelists, he speak to the screaming church ministers that hasn't help the truly poor and retched in a long time; he's speaks to the rich and wealthy and blesses them all with good fortune. Meanwhile here I lay broken in spirit and forgotten and he won't even send an angel in his place to say hi.

I laid in my clothes I've never left out of except to bring food in for my cats and I or to the Pain management program I go to once a month for prescriptions for my neuropathy, but this month I wreaked waiting to hear from God.

Nothing, I thought at first, so I gave up fighting him and accepted my defeat and possible his anger and retribution. I gave in and told God no matter what my life will end up as I will love him unconditionally and guess what a thought was placed in my head to write this letter, in doing so memories flood my mind of all the times God has saved my life and I began to cry tears of repentance and asked God to forgive me, He did.

I've been typing since eight o'clock last night until six am this morning. Whether or not this letter get to where it needs to go, all I know is that suffering for those chosen carries the world hopes in there hearts and minds, for it's through pain that causes the sleeper to awaken and be fully conscious of all that is around them. However, it is the same chosen few that the clarity of mind and spirit drive them insane unable to change the outcome for all life on earth or earth itself.

All I can do is attempting to reach out, to stop the disintegration of humanity; God already let me know it's inevitable. Maybe some souls may be saved through my words through His inspiration and others alike. I may never be rich or get rich materialistically, but God has shown me my riches may lie elsewhere. Thank You El Shaddai.

Pharaoh Xavier author, born in New Jersey, the youngest boy of seven siblings, he has one living parent, his loving mother. Out of his seven siblings, six are married and have blessed their mother with fifteen grand children and ten great grand children. However, Pharaoh never married due to the life experience he went through, he felt that since no one was their especially his father who died when he was just a little child confused about death and the taking away the one staple in his life that could have saved him from the horrors that awaited him.

Printed in the United States
By Bookmasters